"MY STORY IS THE STORY OF MANY GIRLS."

– Malala Yousafzai

Groundwood Books / House of Anansi Press
groundwoodbooks.com

We gratefully acknowledge the Government of Canada for their financial support of our publishing program.

With the participation of the Government of Canada
Avec la participation du gouvernement du Canada   Canadä

Library and Archives Canada Cataloguing in Publication
Title: Malala speaks out / speech by Malala Yousafzai ; commentary by Clara Fons Duocastella ; translation by Susan Ouriou ; illustrations by Yael Frankel.
Other titles: Mi historia es la historia de muchas chicas. English
Names: Fons Duocastella, Clara, author. | container of (Work): Yousafzai, Malala, Nobel lecture. | Yousafzai, Malala, author. | Ouriou, Susan, translator. | Frankel, Yael, illustrator.
Description: Series statement: Speak out series | Translation of: Mi historia es la historia de muchas chicas. | Speech in English; commentary translated from the Spanish.
Identifiers: Canadiana (print) 20220276013 | Canadiana (ebook) 20220276722 | ISBN 9781773069166 (hardcover) | ISBN 9781773069173 (EPUB)
Subjects: LCSH: Yousafzai, Malala, Nobel lecture—Juvenile literature. | LCSH: Girls—Education—Juvenile literature.
Classification: LCC LC1485 .F6613 2023 | DDC j371.822—dc23

On page 19, Malala Yousafzai's name has been written in Pashto by Bakir Eskandari.

The illustrations were created using black pencil and digital media.
Design by Inês Castel-Branco and Danielle Arbour
Printed and bound in South Korea

MALALA
SPEAKS OUT

Speech by Malala Yousafzai | Commentary by Clara Fons Duocastella
Translation by Susan Ouriou | Illustrations by Yael Frankel

GROUNDWOOD BOOKS HOUSE OF ANANSI PRESS TORONTO / BERKELEY

Contents

SPEECH

KEYS TO THE SPEECH

Malala Yousafzai's Nobel Peace Prize Acceptance Speech

Oslo, December 10, 2014

Bismillah hir rahman ir rahim. In the name of God, the most merciful, the most beneficent.

Your Majesties, Your Royal Highnesses, distinguished members of the Norwegian Nobel Committee, dear sisters and brothers: today is a day of great happiness for me. I am humbled that the Nobel Committee has selected me for this precious award.

Thank you to everyone for your continued support and love. Thank you for the letters and cards that I still receive from all around the world. Your kind and encouraging words strengthen and inspire me.

I would like to thank my parents for their unconditional love. Thank you to my father for not clipping my wings and for letting me fly. Thank you to my mother for inspiring me to be patient and to always speak the truth—which we strongly believe is the true message of Islam. And also thank you to all my wonderful teachers, who inspired me to believe in myself and be brave.

"Thank you to my father for not clipping my wings and for letting me fly."

"I am very proud to be the first Pashtun, the first Pakistani, and the youngest person to receive this award."

I am proud, well in fact, I am very proud to be the first Pashtun, the first Pakistani, and the youngest person to receive this award.

Along with that, I am pretty certain that I am also the first recipient of the Nobel Peace Prize who still fights with her younger brothers. I want there to be peace everywhere, but my brothers and I are still working on that.

I am also honored to receive this award together with Kailash Satyarthi, who has been a champion for children's rights for a long time. Twice as long, in fact, than I have been alive. I am proud that we can work together, we can work together and show the world that an Indian and a Pakistani can work together and achieve their goals of children's rights.

Dear brothers and sisters, I was named after the inspirational Malalai of Maiwand who is the Pashtun Joan of Arc. The word Malala means "grief stricken," "sad," but in order to lend some happiness to it, my grandfather would always call me "Malala—The happiest girl in the world." And today I am very happy that we are together fighting for an important cause.

This award is not just for me. It is for those forgotten children who want an education. It is for those frightened children who want peace. It is for those voiceless children who want change.

I am here to stand up for their rights, to raise their voice ... it is not time to pity them. It is time to take action so it becomes the last time that we see a child deprived of education.

"This award is not just for me. ... It is for those voiceless children who want change."

"I am just a committed and even stubborn person who wants to see every child getting quality education."

I have found that people describe me in many different ways.

Some people call me the girl who was shot by the Taliban.

And some, the girl who fought for her rights.

Some people call me a "Nobel Laureate" now.

However, my brothers still call me that annoying bossy sister.

As far as I know, I am just a committed and even stubborn person who wants to see every child getting quality education, who wants to see women having equal rights and who wants peace in every corner of the world.

malala ...

ملاله يوسفزۍ

Education is one of the blessings of life—and one of its necessities. That has been my experience during the seventeen years of my life. In my paradise home, Swat, I always loved learning and discovering new things. I remember when my friends and I would decorate our hands with henna on special occasions. And instead of drawing flowers and patterns we would paint our hands with mathematical formulas and equations.

We had a thirst for education, because our future was right there in that classroom. We would sit and learn and read together. We loved to wear neat and tidy school uniforms and we would sit there with big dreams in our eyes. We wanted to make our parents proud and prove that we could also excel in our studies and achieve those goals, which some people think only boys can.

"Instead of drawing flowers and patterns we would paint our hands with mathematical formulas and equations."

But things did not remain the same. When I was in Swat, which was a place of tourism and beauty, it suddenly changed into a place of terrorism. I was just ten when more than four hundred schools were destroyed. Women were flogged. People were killed. And our beautiful dreams turned into nightmares.

"Our beautiful dreams turned into nightmares."

"I decided to speak up."

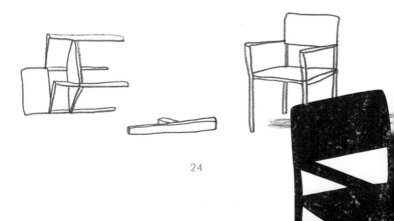

Education went from being a right to being a crime.

Girls were stopped from going to school.

When my world suddenly changed, my priorities changed too.

I had two options. One was to remain silent and wait to be killed. And the second was to speak up and then be killed.

I chose the second one. I decided to speak up.

We could not just stand by and see those injustices of the terrorists denying our rights, ruthlessly killing people and misusing the name of Islam. We decided to raise our voice and tell them: Have you not learnt, have you not learnt that in the Holy Qur'an Allah says, "If you kill one person it is as if you kill all of humanity"?

Do you not know that Mohammad, peace be upon him, the prophet of mercy, he says, "do not harm yourself or others"?

And do you not know that the very first word of the Holy Qur'an is the word "Iqra," which means "read"?

"If you kill one person it is as if you kill all of humanity"?

The terrorists tried to stop us and attacked me and my friends who are here today, on our school bus in 2012, but neither their ideas nor their bullets could win.

We survived. And since that day, our voices have grown louder and louder.

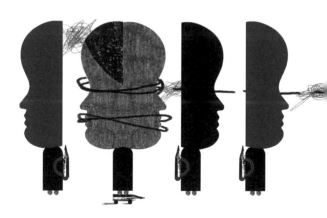

"And since that day, our voices have grown louder and louder."

"I tell my story, not because it is unique, but because it is not."

I tell my story, not because it is unique, but because it is not.

It is the story of many girls.

Today, I tell their stories too. I have brought with me some of my sisters from Pakistan, from Nigeria and from Syria, who share this story. My brave sisters Shazia and Kainat who were also shot that day on our school bus. But they have not stopped learning. And my brave sister Kainat Soomro who went through severe abuse and extreme violence; even her brother was killed, but she did not succumb.

Also my sisters here, whom I have met during my Malala Fund campaign. My sixteen-year-old courageous sister, Mezon from Syria, who now lives in Jordan as a refugee and goes from tent to tent encouraging girls and boys to learn. And my sister Amina, from the North of Nigeria, where Boko Haram threatens, and stops girls and even kidnaps girls, just for wanting to go to school.

Though I appear as one girl, one person, who is 5 foot 2 inches tall, if you include my high heels (it means I am 5 foot only), I am not a lone voice, I am many.

I am Malala. But I am also Shazia.

I am Kainat.

I am Kainat Soomro.

I am Mezon.

I am Amina. I am those 66 million girls who are deprived of education. And today I am not raising my voice, it is the voice of those 66 million girls.

"Though I appear as
one girl, one person ...

I am not a lone voice,
I am many."

Sometimes people like to ask me why should girls go to school, why is it important for them. But I think the more important question is why shouldn't they? Why shouldn't they have this right to go to school?

Dear brothers and sisters, today, in half of the world, we see rapid progress and development. However, there are many countries where millions still suffer from the very old problems of war, poverty and injustice.

We still see conflicts in which innocent people lose their lives and children become orphans. We see many people becoming refugees in Syria, Gaza and Iraq. In Afghanistan, we see families being killed in suicide attacks and bomb blasts.

"People like to ask me why should girls go to school ... the more important question is why shouldn't they?"

Many children in Africa do not have access to education because of poverty. And as I said, we still see girls who have no freedom to go to school in the north of Nigeria.

Many children in countries like Pakistan and India, as Kailash Satyarthi mentioned, many children, especially in India and Pakistan, are deprived of their right to education because of social taboos, or they have been forced into child marriage or into child labor.

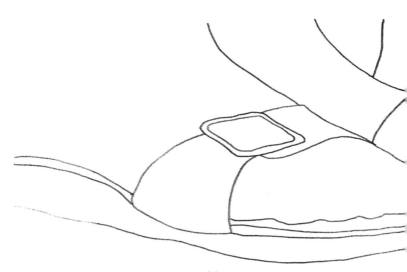

"Many children in countries like Pakistan and India ... are deprived of their right to education because of social taboos."

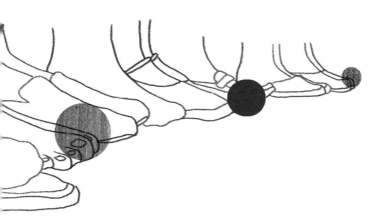

One of my very good school friends, the same age as me, who has always been a bold and confident girl, dreamed of becoming a doctor. But her dream remained a dream. At the age of twelve, she was forced to get married. And then soon she had a son. She had a child when she herself was still a child—only fourteen. I know that she could have been a very good doctor.

But she couldn't ... because she was a girl.

Her story is why I dedicate the Nobel Peace Prize money to the Malala Fund, to help give girls quality education, everywhere, anywhere in the world and to raise their voices. The first place this funding will go to is where my heart is, to build schools in Pakistan—especially in my home of Swat and Shangla.

"The first place this funding will go to is where my heart is, to build schools in Pakistan."

"I will continue to fight until I see every child in school."

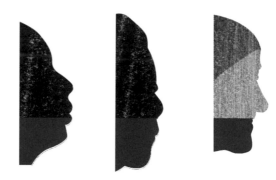

In my own village, there is still no secondary school for girls. And it is my wish and my commitment, and now my challenge to build one so that my friends and my sisters can go to school there and get a quality education and get this opportunity to fulfill their dreams.

This is where I will begin, but it is not where I will stop. I will continue this fight until I see every child in school.

Dear brothers and sisters, great people who brought change, like Martin Luther King and Nelson Mandela, Mother Teresa and Aung San Suu Kyi, once stood here on this stage. I hope the steps that Kailash Satyarthi and I have taken so far and will take on this journey will also bring change—lasting change.

My great hope is that this will be the last time we must fight for education. Let's solve this once and for all.

We have already taken many steps. Now it is time to take a leap.

It is not time to tell the world leaders to realize how important education is—they already know it and their own children are in good schools. Now it is time to call them to take action for the rest of the world's children.

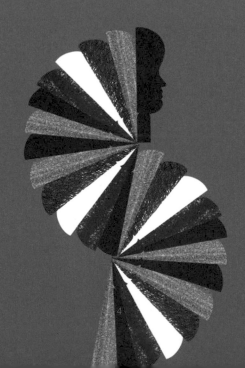

"My great hope is that this will be the last time we must fight for education."

"We ask the world leaders to unite and make education their top priority."

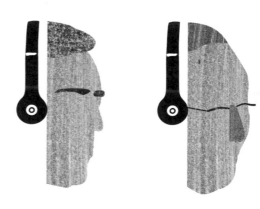

We ask the world leaders to unite and make education their top priority.

Fifteen years ago, the world leaders decided on a set of global goals, the Millennium Development Goals. In the years that have followed, we have seen some progress. The number of children out of school has been halved, as Kailash Satyarthi said. However, the world focused only on primary education, and progress did not reach everyone.

During 2015, representatives from all around the world will meet at the United Nations to set the next set of goals, the Sustainable Development Goals. This will set the world's ambition for the next generations.

The world can no longer accept that basic education is enough. Why do leaders accept that for children in developing countries, only basic literacy is sufficient, when their own children do homework in Algebra, Mathematics, Science and Physics?

Leaders must seize this opportunity to guarantee a free, quality, primary and secondary education for every child.

Some will say this is impractical, or too expensive, or too hard. Or maybe even impossible. But it is time the world thinks bigger.

"The world can no longer accept that basic education is enough."

"Why is it that countries which we call 'strong' are so powerful in creating wars but are so weak in bringing peace?"

Dear sisters and brothers, the so-called world of adults may understand it, but we children don't. Why is it that countries which we call "strong" are so powerful in creating wars but are so weak in bringing peace? Why is it that giving guns is so easy but giving books is so hard? Why is it that making tanks is so easy, but building schools is so hard?

We are living in the modern age and we believe that nothing is impossible. We reached the moon forty-five years ago and maybe we will soon land on Mars. Then, in this 21st century, we must be able to give every child quality education.

Dear sisters and brothers, dear fellow children, we must work ... not wait. Not just the politicians and the world leaders, we all need to contribute. Me. You. We. It is our duty.

Let us become the first generation that decides to be the last that sees empty classrooms, lost childhoods and wasted potentials.

Let this be the last time that a girl or a boy spends their childhood in a factory.

"Let us become the first generation that decides to be the last that sees empty classrooms, lost childhoods and wasted potentials."

Let this be the last time that a girl is forced into early child marriage.

Let this be the last time that a child loses life in war.

Let this be the last time that we see a child out of school.

Let this end with us.

Let's begin this ending ... together ... today ... right here, right now. Let's begin this ending now.

Thank you so much.

"Let's begin this ending now."

KEYS TO THE SPEECH
The Youngest Nobel Peace Prize Laureate in History

Commentary by Clara Fons Duocastella
Translated by Susan Ouriou

On December 10, 2014, in Oslo City Hall (Norway), Malala Yousafzai pronounced the speech reproduced in this book. At seventeen years of age, she became the youngest person ever to receive the Nobel Peace Prize, considered to be the most prestigious honor in the world. She shared the award with Kailash Satyarthi, an Indian activist recognized for his fight for children's rights and against child exploitation. At the time that she received the prize, a death threat issued by the Taliban still hung over Malala, who had yet to fully recover from the many operations that saved her life after the terrorist attack that targeted her for defending girls' education and peace in her country.

Here we will learn who Malala Yousafzai is, what hardships come with living in a country at war, why it is important that everyone be given access to education, how fundamentalism is born and what non-violence is.

Who Is Malala Yousafzai?

On July 12, 1997, the eldest child of Toor Pekai and Ziauddin Yousafzai is born in the town of Mingora, Pakistan. Her parents decide to name her Malala after the great Pashtun heroine Malalai of Maiwand, who, in 1880, inspired the Afghan army to defeat the British in a big battle of the Second Anglo-Afghan War. Their house is a modest building just across from the school that Ziauddin founded with very little money. Malala spends a great deal of time in her father's school and playing with her two brothers, Khushal and Atal, in the surrounding streets. Their favorite game is cricket and, when they can't find a ball, they make one by stuffing an old sock full of odds and ends.

Many people drop by their house: relatives, neighbors, friends and acquaintances. Malala's mother cooks while she talks to the other women, their veils off, revealing bright makeup. Her father and the other men drink tea and talk politics. Malala's mother wears a scarf that hides all of her face except for her eyes; it is called a niqab. Other women wear burqas that cover their whole head, eyes and face. Some even wear gloves and socks to ensure that no part of the body shows.

At a very young age, Malala decided she wouldn't cover her face since she sees it as part of her identity. Already, instead of staying in the kitchen with the women, she prefers sitting at her father's feet and listening to him talk politics with the other men.

Over time, her father founds two other education

facilities in addition to the elementary school: one for girls and another for boys. This brings in a bit more revenue for the family that they share with others: they welcome another family into their home, provide food to those in need and offer scholarships to the children of destitute families.

Up to this point, Malala attends school regularly, earning top marks in her class. However, at only eight, her biggest dream is disrupted with the Taliban's incursion into Swat Valley. With their arrival, a series of activities are forbidden, including girls attending school.

Swat Valley

Swat Valley, famous for its natural beauty, is found in northern Pakistan. The majority of its population is Pashtun. They have their own traditions and define themselves as a proud, hospitable people. The Pashtuns (or Pathan people) speak the Pashto language.

Pakistan—which means "land of the pure"—is located in South Asia. It borders on the Arabian Sea, Iran, China, India and Afghanistan. After decades of British colonial rule, the country gained independence in 1947 through the Partition of the British Indian Empire.

Pakistan is an Islamic republic and does not support the Taliban, an organized violent group with its own interpretation of Islam. The Taliban began instigating attacks against the people in the early 2000s. Pakistan's inhabitants are the victims of Taliban terrorist attacks, as well as attacks by the Pakistan army and of American drones meant to eliminate the Taliban but that also kill, wound and destroy civilian populations.

An Earthquake and Crushing Fear

Malala is eight when, on October 8, 2005, Pakistan suffers one of the worst earthquakes in its history. In the Shangla district, many mountain towns are utterly destroyed, including the towns in which Malala's mother and father were born.

The hardest-hit regions receive immediate assistance from the radical Islamic group Movement for the Enforcement of Islamic Law (Tehreek Nifaz-e-Shariat Mohammadi or TNSM). This is a group that supports the Taliban and was banned in Pakistan in 2002. It is led by Sufi Muhammad and his son-in-law Maulana Fazlullah and plays a crucial role in burying the dead and rebuilding towns. It also takes charge of the thousands of orphaned children, sending them to live in madrasahs (schools of Islamic teaching) where they spend most of their time learning to recite the Qur'an.

TNSM's actions lend credibility to its religious leaders—the mullahs—who claim that the earthquake was a warning from God. They say that if people do not follow the Islamic law governing personal and social conduct, known as Sharia — as interpreted by the mullahs — the punishments will continue.

From that time on, Malala's father faces pressure to close the girls' school. He is told that, in accordance with what the TNSM sees as Islam's straight path, adolescent girls must neither be educated nor be among men.

Soon after, broadcasts begin of Mullah Fazlullah's instructions over the radio: "Pray every day. Stop listening to music, stop going to the movie theater, stop dancing. Stop immediately. If you do not, God will send another earthquake to punish us."

A majority of people start to believe the earthquake was, in fact, an act of divine will. Fazlullah starts to be known as Radio Mullah for the sermons that he gives on his illegal radio station, Mullah FM. The sermons create a climate of fear and coercion by promoting violence, banning girls' education and insisting that women cannot go out unless accompanied by a man.

Speechifying leads to personal attacks, and the names of "sinners"—those who do not follow the Taliban's edicts—are announced over the radio. In short order, girls' schools are banned.

Then sermons over the radio escalate to deeds. People carry television sets, CD and DVD players into town squares to have members of Radio Mullah burn them on site. Women are no longer seen on the streets. Barbers are banned from shaving men's beards. Music stores shut down and families give the mullah money and jewelry to finance the building of bombs and the training of militia. Girls' schools gradually empty and teachers refuse to work there. Numerous public floggings take place and the killing of the Taliban's enemies is constant.

In just one year, 2008, the Taliban bombs over a hundred schools. Some Taliban (wearing explosives that they then detonate) blow themselves up in crowded areas to cause increasing numbers of wounded and dead, and add to the population's fear.

The Pakistan army executes a dramatic military operation meant to put an end to the Taliban's acts of repression. However, the only outcome is more bombing and violence in Swat Valley.

To live with terrorism and war is to live in a permanent state of fear. Who can you trust? Is there such a thing as a safe haven?

A Heroine in Pakistan

It is in the space provided by her beloved Khushal School that Malala can dream and satisfy her preoccupation with learning. For the longest time, it has been an oasis of peace for her and the other girls at the school. As the Taliban's attacks begin, the girls use class time to talk about their experiences with repression.

Malala's courage and her need to express her thoughts and feelings continue to grow, fueled by the example set by her father, who ignores his fear and decries, publicly and continually, the Taliban's actions. When Malala is eleven, the BBC Urdu web service is looking for a girl to write a blog describing life in Pakistan under Taliban rule. Her father eventually puts her name forward after Malala says she wants to do it, and she begins to write under the pseudonym Gul Makai. She titles it *Diary of a Pakistani schoolgirl* and describes and denounces life under Taliban rule.

Malala starts giving interviews and talks. Her speeches are frank and spirited and empower people by not laying responsibility solely at politicians' doors. Although she is soon forced to shut down the blog for reasons of personal safety, Malala has gained visibility and is considered a heroine in her country. Two years later, the Pakistan government creates the National Peace Prize for Youth, the "Malala Prize," in recognition of her work.

The war between the Taliban and Pakistan's military forces Malala and her family to flee Mingora for several months, along with two million other people. It is the greatest exodus in the history of the Pashtun people.

Meanwhile, Malala continues to receive recognition. She is granted many international prizes for her campaign on behalf of girls' rights and peace. Given her visibility and her public denunciation of the Taliban's actions, Malala has become one of their targets. They are determined to kill her.

The Attack

On the afternoon of October 9, 2012, back in Mingora, Malala has just finished an exam and is on her way home on the school bus. She is accompanied by nineteen other girls and two female teachers. It is hot out. Malala chats happily with her best friend, Moniba, and the other girls sing and talk to each other. Suddenly, the vehicle comes to a standstill. Everything is strangely silent! There isn't a soul on the street ...

Two men in white have stepped up to the bus. One asks the driver whether this is the Khushal School bus. Immediately afterward, the other man turns to the passengers and asks, "Which one is Malala?"

Nobody answers, but instinctively a few of the girls turn to look at her. She is the only one not wearing a face covering. Malala squeezes Moniba's hand. The man pulls out a gun and shoots her. Three times. The girls scream. Malala ducks, shielding her head with her hands, but a bullet pierces her skull, passing between her left eyebrow and ear, and travels down her neck to her shoulder. Two other friends, Shazia and Kainat, are also wounded. The bus driver rushes to Swat's main hospital. The Taliban claim responsibility for the attack ordered by Fazlullah.

Malala is close to death, her condition growing more critical by the minute. For that reason, the doctors, with the consent of Malala's father and mother, decide to transfer her to a hospital in the United Kingdom, in Birmingham. Urgently, and in a private jet. News of the attack on one of the most well-known activists in the fight for the right of girls to an education reverberates around the world.

Malala triumphs over multiple operations, treatments and a great deal of pain. It seems like a miracle. A few weeks after she first opens her eyes and says her first words, she is shown letters and postcards from all corners of the planet. Close to eight thousand! All of them messages of support wishing her a speedy recovery. They are written by children, young people, political figures, diplomats, singers, actors ...

There are also packages of gifts, the most precious in her eyes being the one sent by Benazir Bhutto's sons of two shawls that belonged to their mother — Pakistan's late prime minister — who was assassinated in 2007.

While Malala is still in hospital, UNESCO (United Nations Organization for Education, Science and Culture) and Pakistan create the UNESCO Malala Fund for Girls' Right to Education, whose goal is to champion girls' access to education.

In 2013, Malala is discharged from the hospital. She stays on with her family in Birmingham where she resumes her studies. She needs to continue her hospital treatments and, back home, she is still under the Taliban death threat. From Birmingham, she will continue her work on behalf of women.

The Political Arena

On July 12, 2013, which is also her sixteenth birthday, Malala Yousafzai gives a speech at the United Nations' American headquarters before the world's major political leaders. Malala wears one of the shawls sent to the hospital by Benazir Bhutto's sons when she was still fighting for her life.

In October 2007, when Malala was ten, Benazir Bhutto returned to Pakistan at the age of fifty-four, and after almost nine years in self-exile in the United Kingdom and the United Arab Emirates, to run in the 2008 Pakistani election. She was the leader of the opposition, running for her third term as prime minister, and seen as an enemy both by the party in power at the time in Pakistan and by Islamic radical groups. She was the first Muslim woman to lead a Muslim country.

Two months after her return, in her last political rally before thousands of followers, Benazir proclaimed, "I put my life in danger and came here because I feel this country is in danger. People are worried. We will bring the country out of this crisis." As she prepared to leave the venue, waving to the multitude of followers, she was shot several times and died. The terrorist then blew himself up, causing the deaths of more than twenty other people and wounding dozens more.

In a sense, Malala has made the decision to continue Benazir Bhutto's work. And so, on July 12, 2013, she steps up to the lectern in the United Nations headquarters, wearing Bhutto's shawl.

After her speech to the United Nations, Malala is presented with the Amnesty International Ambassador of Conscience Award, the organization's most prestigious distinction. Soon after, she is awarded the European Parliament's Sakharov Prize for Freedom of Thought. In 2014, she receives the Nobel Peace Prize and becomes the youngest laureate ever. In 2017, she is inducted as a United Nations Messenger of Peace and, once again, is the youngest person to receive the honorific title. Several years prior, the UN declared July 12 to be Malala Day. These are only a few of the honors that have come Malala's way worldwide.

The Nobel Peace Prize

On October 10, 2014, the announcement is made that the Nobel Peace Prize is to be awarded to Malala Yousafzai. Two months later, Malala attends the award ceremony and delivers the speech found here.

The ceremony is presided over by Norway's king, queen, princess and prince. Malala is accompanied by her father, mother and brothers, all of whom are visibly happy and moved. She is also accompanied by her friends Shazia and Kainat, who were shot on the bus at the same time as Malala; Kainat Soomro, a Pakistani woman who fought for justice after being sexually assaulted at the age of thirteen; Mezon, a Syrian refugee living in Jordan, who encourages the children in the refugee camp to learn; and Amina from the North of Nigeria, where Boko Haram threatens and abducts girls who go to school.

The Nobel Committee made the conscious decision to simultaneously award the distinction to Malala Yousafzai and Kailash Satyarthi. A teenaged girl and a middle-aged man, one from Pakistan, the other from India, a Muslim and a Hindu, sharing the same honor, was seen as significant by the Nobel committee. Both tireless defenders of children's rights.

Before Malala speaks to the audience, the Nobel committee's chairman hands her the gold medal and diploma awarded to her as a Nobel Peace Prize laureate. With the standing ovations and applause, Malala lays her right hand over her heart in gratitude several times.

At the lectern, Malala adjusts her headscarf and expresses herself fluently while gesturing with her right hand, her direct gaze continually sweeping the audience. In an unhurried, clear and forceful voice, she conveys her passion to those present and is interrupted on several occasions by their lengthy applause.

Throughout her speech, Malala uses several techniques to effectively deliver her message. She puts personal stories front and center. She speaks of her own experience and that of her friends: of using henna to paint equations on their hands, or of one friend who dreamed of becoming a doctor and had to abandon that dream when she was forced into child marriage and into becoming a mother before her time.

This is one way of captivating an audience and conveying a message without subterfuge: "Though I appear as one girl, one person, [...] *I am* not a lone voice. *I am* many. *I am* Malala. But *I am* also Shazia. *I am* Kainat. *I am* Kainat Soomro. *I am* Mezon. *I am* Amina. *I am* those 66 million girls who are deprived of education," she says.

Malala often uses repetition to underline her message: "I am proud that *we can work together, we can work together* and show the world that an Indian and a Pakistani *can work together* and achieve their goals of children's rights." Later, she asserts: "This award is not just for me. *It is for those* forgotten *children* who want an education. *It is for those* frightened *children* who want peace. *It is for those* voiceless *children* who want change."

And near the end of her speech, she starts every sentence in the same way: "*Let this be the last time* that a girl or a boy spends their childhood in a factory. *Let this be the last time that* a girl is forced into early child marriage. *Let this be the last time that* a child loses life in a war. *Let this be the last time that* we see a child out of school." The rhetorical device of repeating the beginning of a phrase is called *anaphora*.

Malala appeals directly to the audience with her gaze as well as with the questions she scatters like seeds throughout, not expecting an answer (*rhetorical questions*): "Why is it that countries which we call 'strong' are so powerful in creating wars but are so weak in bringing peace? Why is it that giving guns is so easy but giving books is so hard? Why is it that making tanks is so easy, but building schools is so hard?"

In her speech, which she often directs to her "dear brothers and sisters," Malala switches back and forth between her personal story and an imperative collective mission on behalf of all humankind.

What Is Fundamentalism?

Malala begins her acceptance speech for the Nobel Peace Prize with this ritual phrase for Muslims: "Bismillah hir rahman ir rahim. In the name of God, the most merciful, the most beneficent."

Malala, as with almost all Pashtuns, is a Sunni Muslim. This means her religion is Islam and her sacred book the Qur'an. From her youngest years, she has communicated with Allah, God, through prayer. When she was only five, every afternoon after school, she would attend a madrasah to study the Qur'an. Malala lives her faith in an open and respectful way.

However, as with any other religion, there are different ways of living one's faith.

Fundamentalism is any movement of organized intolerance that demands strict adherence to inflexible beliefs. It rejects outside influences that run counter to those beliefs. From a philosophical point of view, extremism and fundamentalism are born as a defensive reaction to uncertainty. In practice, this uncertainty is often compounded by political, economic and cultural instability. Fundamentalist groups and people are found in all religions, although the monotheistic religions — such as Christianity, Judaism and Islam — produce the greatest number.

The Taliban are one such fundamentalist group. Fueled by resentment toward the West and the role it has played in the instability of the region, they wage war on any Muslim who does not follow their strictures, like Malala.

She has been clear in voicing her disagreement with various interpretations of Sharia law and with those who misconstrue the concept of jihad (meaning "effort") when they interpret it as the armed struggle against the "enemy" or "nonbelievers." Islam as seen by Malala does not encroach on life or liberty. Islam does not support violence, oppression or the negation of the rights of any person.

Malala's speech ends with these words: "Do you not know that Mohammad, peace be upon him, the prophet mercy, he says, 'do not harm yourself or others'?"

Nonviolence

Malala does not believe in violence as a way of resolving conflict.

In fact, Malala has renounced badal, an idea in Pashto culture that bad behavior should be paid back in kind (i.e., if you steal, you should be stolen from). Sometimes the consequences can be violent, but Malala opposes violence, including violence in the name of justice.

In her speech, Malala refers to Martin Luther King Jr., Nelson Mandela, Mother Teresa and Aung San Suu Kyi, and also highlights the importance of being awarded the prize jointly with Kailash Satyarthi. Thus, Malala, a Muslim girl advocating for change cites as her role models notable figures from other religious traditions, as well as other female figures from her own. Although well aware that no one person is perfect and that those same people, each with her or his own path and convictions, have also made mistakes, she nevertheless recognizes them for having defended their beliefs through nonviolent opposition.

Nonviolence means fighting to bring about change without violence and is carried out with the goal of transforming a situation of conflict.

There are many reasons to reject violence:

• First, ethical reasons: just by existing, every human being has absolute value. Furthermore, what conflict is lessened by another's death? What can be solved by destroying a city?

- Second, rational reasons: when a conflict is resolved through violence, it is almost always the strongest and not necessarily the most just who win. In other words, when violence is involved, there are winners and losers, but no solutions for what might have caused the conflict in the first place.
- Finally, strategic reasons: nonviolent action serves as a "weapon" that can be wielded by the masses and not just by those who have economic or political power. As in, for example, general strikes, sit-ins, marches and protests.

Malala champions nonviolence with deep conviction. She harbors no animosity toward those who tried to kill her. She knows that the Taliban can destroy her body, yet they cannot kill her beliefs, her desires, her dreams ... nor are they capable of silencing the many voices that have been raised on her behalf.

A Girl's Right to Education

For most Pashtuns, the birth of a girl is not celebrated, and in fact only boys' names would be recorded in the clan's genealogical tree. Malala's case was different because her father did not strictly follow the custom.

Despite her father's support and a lifetime spent flouting convention, Malala knew that the simple fact that she was a girl would deprive her of many of the most basic rights and hamper her ability to make decisions.

It was clear that women were expected to stay at home and attend to household chores; even if they did want to pursue a career, they might only be able to study medicine in order to care for other women, or become teachers, but there was almost nothing else they could qualify for.

In Pakistan, the literacy rate is 40 percent. Malala's mother was among the 60 percent that could neither read nor write. (She had been set to start learning the day Malala was shot.) Worldwide, it is estimated that there are 770 million people who are illiterate, and that about two out of every three are women.

Not being literate does not just mean not being able to read or write, it also makes it very difficult to be a citizen who can interact with the world and its institutions, such as the medical system or courts of law.

In response to this situation, in 2013 Malala created the Malala Fund. The fund is premised on the conviction that all children and young people have the ability to change the world if given the opportunity. Hence, the Malala Fund invests in local educators and advocates to make education accessible for girls everywhere. Currently, it has projects in Afghanistan, Pakistan, India, Nigeria, Brazil, Ethiopia, Lebanon and Turkey.

Today, Malala continues to be a tireless advocate for women's rights and the right to an education and to peace. Her mother can now read in both Urdu and English, and her father now participates in household chores. Malala still fights with her brothers on occasion.

In 2018, at the age of twenty and with a large military contingent for protection, she visited Pakistan for the first time since the attack. That same year, the Taliban leader Fazlullah died in Afghanistan during an American air strike.

Malala graduated from Oxford University in 2020 with a degree in Philosophy, Politics and Economics from Lady Margaret Hall — the same college that Benazir Bhutto attended. She is now married and continues to live in the United Kingdom. Malala has said that she hopes to return to Pakistan one day, to encourage everyone to work to create a world that is more just for all.

Dear sisters and brothers, dear fellow children, we must work... not wait. Not just the politicians and the world leaders, we all need to contribute. Me. You. We. It is our duty. ... Let's begin this ending ... together ... today ... right here, right now. Let's begin this ending now.

Source Note

Page 68: "I put my life in danger ..." Benazir Bhutto quoted in "FACTBOX: Benazir Bhutto spoke of dangers ahead of killing" by Reuters Staff, *Reuters*, 27 Dec. 2007.

Further Reading

Yousafzai, Malala and Christina Lamb. *I Am Malala: The Girl Who Stood Up for Education and Was Shot by the Taliban*. New York: Little, Brown and Company, 2013.

Groundwood Books is grateful for the opportunity to share stories and make books on the Traditional Territory of many Nations, including the Anishinabeg, the Wendat and the Haudenosaunee. It is also the Treaty Lands of the Mississaugas of the Credit. In partnership with Indigenous writers, illustrators, editors and translators, we commit to publishing stories that reflect the experiences of Indigenous Peoples. For more about our work and values, visit us at groundwoodbooks.com.